THE TAPESTRY OF EMOTIONS

SOUMYA RANJAN SAHU

INDIA • SINGAPORE • MALAYSIA

ISBN
Hardcase 979-8-89699-933-1
Paperback 979-8-89699-496-1

Dedicated

To all souls who seek understanding, find solace in words, and embrace the beauty in life's struggles and triumphs.

Contents

III
SELF-REFLECTION

IV
RESILIENCE

V
EMOTIONAL TRANSFORMATION

About the Author

Soumya Ranjan Sahu *is a passionate poet, first-time author, and judicial aspirant whose work delves deeply into the themes of love, loss, resilience, and self-discovery. Born with physical challenges, Soumya has always sought solace in writing, finding it to be a powerful way to navigate the complexities of emotions and connect with others on a profound level. For him, poetry has been more than just an art form—it has been a means of expression, healing, and finding peace in a world that often feels uncertain.*

Soumya's poems are a reflection of his personal experiences, but they resonate with anyone who has faced heartache, triumph, or moments of deep introspection. His writing captures both the fragility and strength of the human spirit, exploring the bittersweet beauty of love, the depth of grief, and the courage to heal. The vulnerability in his words speaks to the universal journey of self-discovery, a theme that runs throughout his collection Echoes of the Heart.

Alongside his creative journey, Soumya is dedicated to pursuing a career in law, driven by a desire to serve justice and make a meaningful difference in society. As a judicial aspirant, he believes that the principles of law and poetry share a common goal— to seek truth, give voice to the voiceless, and encourage empathy and understanding. His legal studies, intertwined with his poetic pursuits, have shaped him into someone who values the power of both knowledge and art to inspire change.

Soumya's love for writing is matched only by his commitment to his aspirations. Whether he is immersed in the pages of a legal textbook or crafting verses that capture the essence of his emotions, he remains driven by a passion to leave a lasting impact. Residing in Odisha, India, Soumya continues to draw inspiration from the beauty of nature, the wisdom found in life's quiet moments, and his unwavering belief in the potential of both justice and creative expression to change the world.

When he is not writing or preparing for his judicial exams, Soumya enjoys reflecting on the simple things in life—meaningful conversations, nature's serene landscapes, and the profound truths that emerge from introspection. His poetry is an invitation to explore the emotional depth of life, offering readers a chance to connect with their own journeys of healing, growth, and resilience.

> **"To write is to embrace life with open arms, even in its most bittersweet moments."**
>
> *– Soumya Ranjan Sahu*

Preface

Poetry, for me, has always been a way to explore the unspoken emotions that lie within us. It is a canvas for love, pain, hope, and self-discovery—a mirror reflecting the deepest corners of the soul. This collection, The Tapestry of Emotion, is a journey through the intricacies of human emotions, drawn from moments of joy, heartbreak, and resilience.

Each poem in this book carries a piece of my own story, woven with the threads of imagination and vulnerability. As a first-time writer and a physically challenged person, I have often found solace in the act of creating. It is through words that I learned to navigate the challenges of life, and it is through poetry that I found my voice.

These verses are not just about my experiences; they are about all of us. They are for anyone who has loved and lost, dreamed and despaired, or sought light in the shadows. My hope is that these poems resonate with you, offering comfort, inspiration, and perhaps a sense of companionship in your own journey.

Thank you for letting me share these pieces of my heart with you. I invite you to immerse yourself in the words and find meaning in their echoes.

With gratitude,
Soumya Ranjan Sahu

I

LOVE

Echoes in the Silence

In the silence of my nights,
Your laughter still lingers, soft and light.
A melody etched upon the air,
A fleeting joy, beyond compare.

The shadows dance, the stars remain,
But nothing soothes this aching pain.
For in the echoes, I find you near,
A phantom voice I long to hear.

Time moves forward, yet stands still,
Your memory bends it to its will.
Each moment whispers your refrain,
A bittersweet and tender pain.

I reach for you in dreams that fade,
Through twilight's veil, where we once stayed.
But dawn arrives, and you're not there,
Just laughter woven in the air.

In the silence of my nights, I dwell,
With secrets only echoes tell.
A love that lingers, pure and true,
Forever bound to the sound of you.

Standing in the Rain

It's like standing in the rain,
No umbrella, just the pain.
Nine long years, yet you remain,
A shadow I can't explain.

Misunderstanding built a wall,
But your presence still calls.
Through silence, through all the strain,
I miss you more, in the rain.

Time has passed, but wounds still stay,
A quiet longing that won't fade away.
Though we're apart, through night and day,
I stand in the rain, hoping you'll stay.

In every drop, a memory falls,
A wish that time would heed my calls.
I miss you still, through joy and strain,
I'll always stand here, in the rain.

The Crime of Love

My heart's only crime, so pure, so true,
Is loving you, as I always do.
A silent plea, a whispered vow,
To serve a lifetime, here and now.

For in this love, there is no wrong,
Just a melody, a lifelong song.
Though it binds me, it sets me free,
In loving you, I cease to be.

No punishment can change my fate,
For loving you, I'll always wait.
A crime, perhaps, but worth the cost,
In your heart, I am never lost.

The Ocean of Love

Sometimes, you give an ocean of love,
A vast, uncharted sea, deep and above.
With currents strong and tides that flow,
You offer all you are, all you know.

But some will stand on the shore so near,
Afraid of the depth, too blind to hear,
The whispers of waves that kiss the sand,
Unable to grasp what you truly planned.

You give them oceans, they touch the shore,
Unaware of the treasures you have in store.
And in the end, they never dive,
Too shallow to feel, too distant to thrive.

But love, like the sea, is endless and wide,
And in its depths, you'll always reside.

Love in Letting Go

In the end, I chose her smile,
Though it broke my heart all the while.
Her joy became my quiet prayer,
A fragile light I chose to bear.

I traded my longing, my deepest ache,
For the laughter her freedom would make.
For love is not a tethered plea,
But the courage to set her free.

To hold her happiness above my own,
To walk away, though I'm alone.
For what is love, if not the art,
Of giving all, even your heart?

And so I loved her, pure and true,
Enough to leave, though it tore me in two.

The Purest Love

The greatest act of love, they say,
Is not to hold, but give away.
To free the wings that long to soar,
Even if they return no more.

For love is not a binding chain,
Nor a tether born of selfish pain.
It's the courage to step aside,
And watch their soul in freedom glide.

To see them grow, to let them be,
The person they are destined to see.
Even if it means you stand apart,
With quiet ache within your heart.

True love endures, though paths divide,
A silent strength, a selfless pride.
For loving wholly is to release,
And find in letting go, your peace.

A Beautiful Reminder

The pain of missing you, so deep,
It lingers softly as I weep.
Yet in this ache, a truth shines through,
The joy of life was loving you.

Each tear becomes a tender thread,
That ties me to the words we said.
No sorrow dark can steal away,
The light you brought to every day.

Your absence carves a hollow space,
Yet fills my heart with endless grace.
For every moment, near or far,
You are my guide, my northern star.

And though this longing feels so near,
It whispers love that conquers fear.
A bittersweet, eternal truth:
To miss is proof of joy, of you.

A Smile that Stays

The moment your smile found its way to me,
A quiet world stirred, like waves in the sea.
No words were spoken, no vows were made,
Yet in that glance, my heart obeyed.

A thread unseen began to entwine,
Binding your soul to the depths of mine.
An unspoken promise, fragile yet strong,
A melody whispered, a lifelong song.

But fear lingers where love takes hold,
Of losing the warmth, the story untold.
If your light should fade, if you drift away,
What's left of my sky would turn to gray?

So here I stand, with hope that burns,
Praying your smile forever returns.
For a bond like this, so rare, so true,
Would leave me longing, eternally, for you.

Whisper in the Void

In the empty room of souls,
Where silence weaves its shrouded scrolls,
Your whisper lingers, soft and clear,
A ghostly hymn I hold so dear.

No walls can cage, no time erase,
The fleeting echo of your grace.
A fleeting touch, a shadowed trace,
A memory carved in boundless space.

Though the room may seem forlorn,
Its quiet pulse forever worn,
Your voice—a thread through endless seams,
A tether to forgotten dreams.

In the void where souls retreat,
Your whisper makes my world complete.

A Beautiful Mistake

Love, a spark in the quiet night,
A fleeting star in endless flight.
It burns so bright, then fades away,
A dream we touch but cannot stay.

A whispered vow, a tender ache,
A fleeting, beautiful mistake.
It leaves its mark, both sweet and sore,
A song that fades yet lingers more.

Though dreams may end, their traces stay,
Etched on hearts in a timeless way.
For love, though brief, its gentle bloom,
Paints our lives in vibrant hues.

When Love isn't Love

You'll know it's not love, deep inside,
When doubt becomes your constant guide.
When whispers of truth you try to drown,
And wear a smile to mask the frown.

Love doesn't ask for proof or plea,
It flows unbound, wild, and free.
It speaks in silence, it needs no voice,
It isn't a question—it's a choice.

If you must convince your heart it's true,
Then love is not what's holding you.
For real love stays, it doesn't pretend,
A flame that warms, not one to mend.

So heed the ache, let falsehood part,
And leave room for a genuine heart

I Will Remember

I know you've forgotten me,
But I'll carry you within my heart,
Through every sunrise, every breeze,
You'll remain, though we're apart.

The world may fade, the years may fly,
And time will wear its marks on me,
But in the quiet of each sigh,
I'll remember you, endlessly.

When shadows fall and nights are long,
Your memory will softly gleam,
A melody, a whispered song,
That dances gently through my dreams.

Though you may not recall my name,
My soul will keep its steady beat,
For in my heart, you'll stay the same,
And I'll remember, incomplete.

II

LOSS

Unbroken Heart

They shattered all I once held dear,
Yet in the ruins, I find no fear.
The pain they caused, the wounds they made,
But love within, will never fade.

I should despise, with anger's flame,
But peace remains, I won't play the game.
For in forgiveness, I rise above,
And carry forth, a heart of love.

The world may break and hearts may tear,
But softness proves the strength I wear.
No bitterness can dim my light,
For I choose grace, and not the fight.

In letting go, I find my way,
A soul reborn with each new day
For in this heart, still soft and free,
I find the power to simply be.

Hard to Love, Easy to Leave

Maybe I'm just hard to hold,
A story untold, too wild, too bold
With walls that rise and hearts that break,
A silent cry that none can take.

I push away what I desire,
Afraid that love might fade, expire.
And so I stand, too hard to see,
A soul both yearning and set free.

Perhaps I'm easy to walk away,
A shadow that slips, then fades to gray.
Yet in this space, I still believe,
That someday, love will find me, weave.

For though I seem so hard to find,
A softer heart still hides behind.
And maybe, just maybe, in time I'll see,
That love can stay, and set me free.

The Ship I Didn't Build

I should have carved you from stars and flame,
A vessel unyielding, worthy of your name.
But I crafted with fear, my grip too tight,
And left you adrift in a world of night.

The compass I gave spun wild with doubt,
Its fractured needle could not map out.
The sails were thin, stitched with despair,
And the winds tore through as if I weren't there.

Yet still, you rise where storms conspire,
Your heart a beacon, your will on fire.
The ship may break, its pieces worn,
But your spirit outlives what I left torn.

You are the sea's defiance, the storm's great plea,
A force too boundless for the likes of me

Ashes of a Wildfire

Your love was a wildfire,
Unstoppable, fierce, and bright,
It burned with a passion so pure,
Illuminating my darkest night.

But now, the flames have faded,
The embers are all that remain,
And though they once held warmth,
It's only ashes that bring me pain.

The fire once freed me,
But now it confines my soul,
What once was wild and freeing,
Now leaves me feeling whole, yet cold.

I choke on the memories,
The smoke of what used to be,
Your love was a fierce inferno,
But the ashes are all that's left of me.

The Paradox of Letting Go

To forget a love so deeply sown,
Is like chasing winds you've never known.
A fleeting shadow, a whispered name,
A heart's soft ache, an eternal flame.

Each memory clings, a stubborn trace,
A ghostly touch, a fleeting face.
The more you run, the more it stays,
A timeless dance through endless days.

To bury love is a futile quest,
It lives unbidden within your chest.
A gentle ache, a silent cry,
A love that lingers, though you try.

Yet in its echo, life will bloom,
From sorrow's shade to light's new room.
For love once felt is never lost,
It shapes the soul, no matter the cost.

A Story Without an Ending

It's better, they say, to never begin,
Than write a tale where none can win.
A story paused, a thread untied,
A hollow ache where hope once lied.

The pages linger, blank and bare,
No whispers soft, no memories there.
Yet emptiness, though hard to bear,
Outweighs the weight of love's despair.

For tales that end in broken time,
Leave echoes lost, an unkept rhyme.
A silence deep, a chasm wide,
Where dreams and truths no more collide.

So let no ink on paper stay,
If hearts must falter, fade away.
For some would choose the void to keep,
Then stories told that end in grief.

Unheard Echoes

Unrequited love is screaming like in a vacuum,
A voice that echoes, but no one hears the tune.
Words collide with silence, shattered and consumed,
In the emptiness, a heart is left to swoon.

I reach for you, but find the space between,
A chasm so vast, no bridge can span the seam.
Your eyes are distant, as if I'm unseen,
Yet my soul bleeds in places you've never dreamed.

I whisper in shadows, hoping you might care,
But my breath fades away in the stagnant air.
Every glance I give, a prayer, a silent dare,
But you're a storm I can't begin to share.

Still, my heart beats with an echoing cry,
Faint, yet unwavering, beneath the darkened sky.
Unrequited love, though unseen, will not die,
It lives in the silence, reaching for the sky.

Drowning in Silence

Loving you feels like drowning in a sea of hope,
Where every breath is a struggle, every wave a plea.
I try to swim, to stay afloat in this endless tide,
But with each stroke, I sink deeper into what could never be.

You don't see me, not in the way I've hoped,
And still, I keep treading, pretending the water's fine.
I smile through the ache, hiding the weight of what I feel,
As if the act of swimming could somehow make this mine.

The distance between us is a current I cannot fight,
Yet I fight it anyway, desperate to be seen.
Each moment of silence a reminder of my own quiet despair,
But I keep swimming, as if your gaze is all I need to breathe.

It's like drowning, but pretending the waters are clear,
Holding on to the dream that you might one day notice.
But in this ocean, I am alone with my love,
Drowning in the silence, hoping for a chance to breathe.

III
SELF-REFLECTION

Flicker of Hope

Born into a world with unseen chains,
A quiet battle, hidden pains.
The days slip by like fading light,
Yet shadows linger, never quite right.

Once I had dreams, vibrant and clear,
Now echoes of them disappear.
I stand in silence, the path unclear,
As each step trembles, gripped by fear.

I've lost what most would hold so dear,
Yet in this stillness, I persevere.
Though the body weakens, the spirit remains,
A quiet strength that bears the strains.

No longer chasing what once was bright,
I've learned to find solace in the night.
For even in the darkest of days,
Hope still flickers in the quiet haze.

Whispers of Time

Time will pass, and dreams will break,
People will leave, but hearts will wake.
With every loss, a lesson's found,
In silence, wisdom does resound.

The fleeting moments slip away,
But in their wake, we learn to stay.
Through joy and pain, we find our way,
New truths arise with each new day.

So let the world change as it may,
For in its turn, we learn and sway.
Through every step, we grow anew,
And life's great lessons will shine through.

The Weight of Memory

I cannot tell what hurts me more,
To hold each moment I adore,
The echoes loud, the shadows near,
The joy, the pain, the whispered tear.

Or to let it fade, a fading hue,
A life I lived, but never knew.
To lose the faces, the voices, the call,
What's worse: to remember or forget it all?

One clings like thorns, a bittersweet bind,
The other, a void that haunts the mind.
Between these truths, my heart is torn,
In love's great loss, I'm both reborn and worn.

The Mirror of My Soul

In the quiet of the morning light,
I look within, not at my face,
But at the soul that hides from sight,
A place of truth, a sacred space.

The world reflects in fractured glass,
But deeper still, I seek the core,
Where judgments fade and shadows pass,
And I, at last, begin to soar.

What lessons hide in this quietude,
Where answers rise from stillness deep?
I seek to know my darkest mood,
And, in the knowing, I shall leap.

So here I stand, both weak and strong,
A soul that learns where I belong.

Fragments of Me

In every step I take, I find,
A fragment lost along the way,
A piece of me, a secret mind,
A memory that longs to stay.

I gather these scattered parts,
A mosaic built on fractured time,
To understand my broken heart,
And hear my voice in whispered rhyme.

Through every scar and every flaw,
I see the whole, though split in two,
The pieces held by nature's law,
That teaches me to be anew.

I am not perfect, yet I rise,
To meet myself beyond the skies.

The Journey Within

I travel far, yet not without,
For every road I choose to roam,
The inner journey calls, no doubt,
To guide me back, to guide me home.

The world outside may change its hue,
But what lies still is who I am,
A wanderer in skies of blue,
A soul entwined in love's own plan.

With every choice, with every sigh,
I pause to question what I see,
And look within, where answers lie,
In the quiet depths of me.

So onward still, I walk with grace,
Embracing each and every place.

The Light of Reflection

I stand in light, but not the sun,
It's light from within, where shadows run,
A truth I see, a truth I seek,
A vision of me, both strong and weak.

The path ahead is not too clear,
But through the fog, I will not fear,
For in my heart, I find the light,
That guides me through the darkest night.

Reflection brings me to my knees,
A humble soul that yearns to see,
The beauty found in self-deep grace,
A truth that shines through time and space.

So let me walk this path of light,
And find in me my inner sight.

The Measure of Life

In the end, it's not the years that stay,
Not the ticking clock or the fleeting day,
But the laughter shared, the love you gave,
The moments you chose to be bold, not brave.

The life in your years is a quiet fire,
A song unsung, yet climbing higher,
It's the tears that fell, the dreams that soared,
The heart you opened, the soul restored.

For time is a thief with a gentle hand,
It slips through fingers like grains of sand,
But a life well-lived leaves traces behind,
In the hearts you touched, the ties that bind.

So don't just count the days you've spent,
But the ones where your spirit leapt and bent,
For it's not the years in your life that matter,
But the life in your years that shapes the chatter

Walls of the Heart

The heart, a fortress, yearning for embrace,
Seeks solace in the warmth of a kindred face.
Yet trembling, it builds walls high and steep,
Guarding wounds it silently keeps.

Oh, the craving for closeness, tender and true,
A bond where trust blooms and skies turn blue.
Yet shadows of pain whisper, "Beware,"
And fear holds its hand with delicate care.

Through cracks in the wall, light dares to stream,
Kindness and love weave into its dream.
A human heart, though fragile, is brave,
In its chambers, a yearning for life to save.

To live is to risk, to heal is to try,
To embrace both laughter and the tears we cry.
For the walls that protect may also confine,
The heart must leap to let its light shine.

IV
RESILIENCE

Melting the Ice

We wander cold, through frozen years,
A heart encased in quiet fears.
The world seems still, a distant hue,
No warmth to touch, no light breaks through.

Yet comes a spark, a gentle flame,
A voice that softly calls your name.
Its heat dissolves the walls of frost,
Reviving all you thought was lost.

You never knew how numb you'd grown,
Until their warmth became your own.
A melting touch, a tender glow,
Unlocking love you dared not show.

And as the ice begins to fade,
You see the life their warmth has made.
A heart unbound, no longer cold,
Awake to love, and brave, and bold.

When Forever Changes

People change when you believe,
They're the ones you'll never leave.
Just when your heart begins to trust,
They fade away, as all things must.

You hold them close, you dream of more,
Of shared tomorrows, hearts to soar.
But time, like shadows, pulls them far,
And love's bright flame turns to a scar.

The ones you thought would always stay,
Slip through your hands, they fade away.
And in the silence, you will see,
That forever's not what it used to be.

Yet in the change, you find your strength,
To rise again, to go the length.
For love is never just one name,
It's how we learn, through loss, through change.

In the Embrace of Shadows

No sun can fill your heart, you know,
When you've chosen to love the dark.
It's not that you want to feel this low,
But something in the shadows left a mark.

You walk with ghosts, yet you stay still,
Caught between the past and what could be.
The light may call, but you won't heal,
For in the dark, you still feel free.

The warmth of day can't touch the space
Where hurt has made its quiet home.
You wish for peace, but there's no grace—
Just echoes in the places you roam.

And though the stars don't light the way,
You've learned to see the beauty here.
In shadows, you've found a place to stay,
A love that's lived without the fear.

Sin of Loving You

I was cursed with the sin of loving you,
A burden sweet, yet sharp and true,
Each whispered name, a heavy chain,
Yet I wear it proud, this sacred pain.

Your shadow lingers in my heart,
A masterpiece of broken art,
Each memory burns, but still I hold,
A fire too fierce, yet soft and cold.

Blessed am I by love's cruel sting,
A melody of sorrowed strings,
For in this ache, I find my peace,
A love unbound, that will not cease.

So let me bear this fated curse,
To love you, still, for better or worse.

In the Hollow Chambers

In the hollow chambers of my heart,
Your absence beats, a piercing dart.
Louder than your presence ever spoke,
A silent ache that leaves me broke.

The echoes linger, sharp and clear,
A symphony of what's not near.
Each pulse a memory, raw and bare,
A rhythm soaked in cold despair.

Once, your voice was my refrain,
A melody to drown the pain.
Now silence reigns, a solemn king,
Each breath a song of suffering.

Yet in this void, I start to see,
A space where healing waits for me.
For absence shapes the heart anew,
And carves a path to wander through.

The Weight of Longing

I carry the weight of a silent plea,
A yearning for something I cannot see.
It whispers softly, calling my name,
Yet I retreat, consumed by shame.

I crave the warmth of an outstretched hand,
A solace I fear I won't withstand.
Each step toward it, I hesitate, pause,
Bound by fear, held by unseen claws.

In pushing it away, I find no peace,
The ache within refuses to cease.
For what I desire is not far, yet near,
A fragile hope, eclipsed by fear.

Oh, to break these chains, to let it stay,
To welcome the light I keep at bay.
For the heart must trust, must learn to fight,
To claim its longing and find the light.

The Battle Within

The mind whispers reason, calm and steady,
A voice that tries to anchor me in truth.
It speaks of logic, of clear paths forward,
Guiding me through storms, promising proof.

But the heart—oh, the heart is louder still,
It screams of chaos, wild and untamed.
It pulls me in directions unknown,
Tugging at my soul, unashamed.

The mind calls for peace, for quiet thought,
But the heart thrives in the mess of emotions.
It craves the chaos, the thrill of the unknown,
As if uncertainty holds the deepest devotion.

I stand between them, torn and confused,
The mind seeking order, the heart a storm.
And in this clash, I find no easy answers,
Only the struggle to be true to both forms.

V

EMOTIONAL TRANSFORMATION

When New Bonds Form

We walked as one, through days gone by,
Our laughter bright beneath the sky.
But seasons change, as do the hearts,
And gently, softly, old ties part.

A new light shines, a path unknown,
Its warmth a call, its seeds are sown.
The threads of us begin to fray,
As newer hands now guide the way.

Yet what we had still holds its glow,
A cherished past we'll always know.
No bitter end, just time's embrace,
To weave anew in love's vast space.

For bonds may shift, yet love remains,
In echoes, dreams, and softened pains.
When new bonds form, the heart expands,
To hold the past with open hands.

Unspoken Bonds

Some people won't understand your words,
They seek meaning where none occurs.
While others feel, without a sound,
The language of your soul profound.

In silence, hearts may intertwine,
A connection deeper than design.
For words are fleeting, love is true,
In whispers felt, without a cue.

No need for speech, no need for voice,
When hearts aligned make the choice.
In every glance, in every sigh,
Unspoken bonds will never die.

Through the quiet, we find our way,
Where love speaks louder than what we say.
In stillness, a truth we learn:
The unspoken is where hearts return.

The Door I Can't Open

Happiness knocks softly, a familiar sound,
Promising warmth, a moment of peace.
But every time, I hesitate, my hands frozen,
For guilt stands beside me, never to cease.

It whispers of mistakes I've yet to make right,
Of promises broken, of things left undone.
And though joy calls to me with open arms,
I stay behind the door, where shadows run.

I feel the weight of the past on my chest,
Each memory a chain that holds me tight.
The joy outside is just out of reach,
But guilt, like a prisoner, controls my night.

How can I embrace what feels so far away,
When the past insists on having its say?
Happiness knocks, but guilt is too loud,
So I remain silent, alone in the crowd.

The Paradox of Healing

In the same breath, I long to heal,
To shed the weight of every scar.
But each wound, though painful, feels like a part of me,
A story written in the lines that shape who I am so far.

I crave the peace that comes with release,
A freedom from the ghosts that linger near.
Yet there's a part of me that clings to the pain,
As if without it, I would disappear.

Healing feels like stepping into the unknown,
A journey toward a self I can't yet see.
But the wounds I carry are my constant companions,
And letting go means losing the only version of me I've come to be.

I stand torn between the hope of a future unscarred,
And the comfort of the past that holds me tight.
For in this struggle, I find my truth:
Healing and holding on are both a fight.

The Quiet Dilemma

I seek solitude, a quiet refuge from the noise,
Hoping for peace in the absence of the world.
In the stillness, I long to find myself,
To heal from the chaos, to feel unfurled.

But when the world fades and silence takes hold,
Loneliness creeps in, colder than the night.
I find no comfort in the quiet I sought,
Only the echo of my own silent fight.

The solitude I crave becomes my cage,
A space where time drips like falling rain.
And though I long for a break from it all,
I find only emptiness, and more pain.

So I walk this line, caught between the two,
Yearning for peace, yet afraid to be free.
For solitude brings a bitter truth with it—
That sometimes, being alone is all we can be.

A Ship at the Airport

Loving you feels like a dream,
A fleeting hope, a distant gleam.
Yet every sign, so loud, so clear,
Reminds me you are nowhere near.

I wait where skies embrace the land,
For sails that seas will not command.
A ship I chase that cannot soar,
Lost in a place it's meant to ignore.

Each moment clings, a heavy chain,
Of endless hope and quiet pain.
Yet still I stand, though reason fades,
Lost in the love my heart has made.

But love unreturned, though pure it seems,
Is bound to break the strongest dreams.
For waiting here, where none arrive,
Leaves only echoes of love contrived.

The Bitter Taste of Words

I wish they could drink their words,
Sip the venom in the verse they've stirred.
Taste the bitterness, raw and true,
And feel the sting of what they spew.

For words, once spoken, cannot fade,
They leave a mark, a silent blade.
Yet if they could taste the poison poured,
Maybe they'd choose their speech more assured.

To swallow the weight of every lie,
And feel the burn of every cry.
Perhaps then, they'd pause, reflect,
On the harm their words might reflect.

But until they learn to taste their own,
The bitterness will stand alone.

The Heart's Journey

The heart, a vessel wild and free,
It drifts upon love's restless sea.
Yet often seeks a fleeting spark,
A flame that fades within the dark.

It beats for those who will not stay,
Who turn and tread a distant way.
Yet in the ache, a truth is spun,
That love is vast, not bound to one.

The tender scars, they softly speak,
Of moments lost, of hearts grown weak.
But in the pain, new strength is sown,
A lesson learned, a wisdom grown.

For though the heart may sometimes stray,
It finds its path, its destined way.
And through the sorrow, it will see,
That love begins with loving thee.

Endless Dreams

If reality cannot compare,
To dreams of you beyond the air,
Then let me drift where shadows gleam,
And lose myself within the dream.

In waking hours, the world feels cold,
Its stories cruel, its moments bold.
But in my dreams, your touch is near,
Your voice, a melody I hear.

No bounds exist, no time to part,
In dreams, I hold your fleeting heart.
A realm where love is pure and true,
And every star leads me to you.

So let me sleep, let night unfold,
A canvas vast, with dreams untold.
If life can't grant this tender plea,
Then let me dream eternally.

The Weight of Silence

I stand alone, but not alone,
The voices whisper in my mind,
Of past mistakes, of seeds I've sown,
The truths I seek, but cannot find.

Each silent moment feels so loud,
A cacophony of self-doubt's call,
Yet through the fog, I stand unbowed,
Learning to rise, though I may fall.

Reflections grow in quiet skies,
Where I confront the hurt I've known,
And with each tear that softly dries,
I find my strength in being grown.

The weight of silence brings me peace,
In stillness, I find my release.

Do Not Speak of Love

If hurting me brings you no pain,
Your love, it feels a hollow claim.
For words mean little, pale and weak,
When actions show the truth you speak.

Do not profess what you can't feel,
Love isn't words; it's what is real.
If breaking me leaves you unscarred,
Your love is but a false façade.

True love will ache when others bleed,
It stands with care, it meets their need.
But if my tears don't reach your soul,
Then love is not your heart's true goal.

So spare me lies and let me be,
Don't speak of love that's void of me.
For love that doesn't feel my pain,
Is not a love, but selfish gain.

Thank You

To my dear readers,

I am deeply grateful for your support and for taking the time to immerse yourself in the pages of this book. Every word, every verse, has been written with love, passion, and the hope that it resonates with your heart. Your encouragement and belief in my work have meant more to me than words can express.

This collection is not just a reflection of my thoughts, but a shared experience that binds us through emotions, stories, and moments. I dedicate this book to all who have inspired, loved, and walked alongside me in this journey. Thank you for your continued belief in the power of words and for being part of this adventure.

With all my gratitude and warmth,
Soumya Ranjan Sahu

www.ingramcontent.com/pod-product-compliance
Lightning Source LLC
LaVergne TN
LVHW091228150826
845673LV00003B/1060

9798896994961